Date: 9/21/17

J BIO NEWTON
Gitlin, Marty,
Cam Newton : football star /

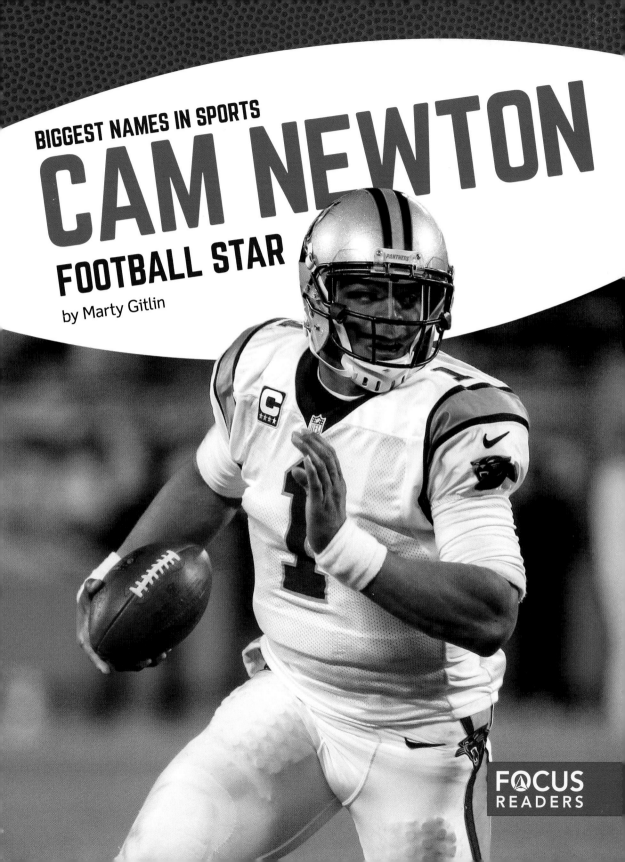

Biggest Names in Sports

CAM NEWTON

FOOTBALL STAR

by Marty Gitlin

FOCUS READERS

WWW.NORTHSTAREDITIONS.COM

Produced for North Star Editions by Red Line Editorial.

Photographs ©: Peter Read Miller/AP Images, cover, 1, 8; Damian Strohmeyer/AP Images, 4–5, 7; Butch Dill/AP Images, 10–11; Tim Casey/University of Florida/Collegiate Images/Getty Images, 13; Black Russian Studio/Shutterstock Images, 15; Action Sports Photography/Shutterstock Images, 16–17; Kent Smith/AP Images, 19; Chuck Burton/AP Images, 20; Phalen M. Ebenhack/AP Images, 22–23; Paul Spinelli/AP Images, 25; Todd Rosenberg/AP Images, 26; Red Line Editorial, 29

ISBN
978-1-63517-044-3 (hardcover)
978-1-63517-100-6 (paperback)
978-1-63517-202-7 (ebook pdf)
978-1-63517-152-5 (hosted ebook)

Library of Congress Control Number: 2016951021

Printed in the United States of America
Mankato, MN
November, 2016

ABOUT THE AUTHOR

Marty Gitlin is a sportswriter and educational book author based in Cleveland, Ohio. He has had more than 100 books published, including dozens about famous athletes.

TABLE OF CONTENTS

CHAPTER 1

SUPERMAN OR SUPER CAM?

The Carolina Panthers were battling the Arizona Cardinals in the National Football Conference (NFC) Championship Game after the 2015 season. The game was still in its third quarter. But it was already clear the Cardinals didn't stand much of a chance. Carolina quarterback Cam Newton had all but buried them.

Cam Newton leaps into the end zone against the Arizona Cardinals.

The Panthers led 27–7. They were 13 yards away from another touchdown. Newton grabbed the snap from center. He took off to the right and broke a tackle. Then he sped up and burst through a hole. Arizona defenders closed in. But Newton would not be denied. He leaped into the end zone for a touchdown.

Newton was not done playing hero. He showed his amazing talents again in the fourth quarter. He lofted a perfect pass to tight end Greg Olsen for 54 yards. He ran up the middle for 14 yards. Then he fired a strike to wide receiver Devin Funchess for a 5-yard touchdown.

Newton and the crowd get fired up before the NFC Championship Game.

The Panthers had clinched the victory. They were the NFC champions, and the team was headed to the Super Bowl.

Newton had an amazing game against the Cardinals. He threw two touchdown passes and ran for two more scores.

Newton beat the Cardinals with his passing and his running.

But those numbers could not define what he meant to his team that day. He proved that he was their leader.

Carolina eventually lost to the Denver Broncos in the Super Bowl. But people didn't forget the amazing season Super Cam had put together. Newton became the first Carolina player to be named the Most Valuable Player (MVP) of the National Football League (NFL). He was the top pick of 48 of the 50 MVP voters.

SUPER CAM

Early in his career, Newton coined a touchdown celebration fit for a superhero. When the comic book character Clark Kent rips off his shirt, he reveals a Superman logo on his chest. When Newton scores a touchdown, he pretends to do the same. Some opponents and fans don't like it. They think it shows arrogance. But Newton's fans and teammates love it.

CHAPTER 2

BUMPY ROAD TO GREATNESS

Cam Newton needed more than talent to succeed. Caring parents also played a big role in his life. Cam, who grew up in Atlanta, Georgia, had strict parents. His mother, Jackie, would not wait for Cam to return home when he behaved badly in school. She would go to the school to punish him.

Cam Newton's hard work paid off when he enrolled at Auburn University.

Cam's father, Cecil, would not allow him to goof around on Saturdays. Cecil made his son work to earn money. The **discipline** and work ethic his parents instilled in him paid off in high school. Cam earned a spot on the **varsity** football team as a freshman.

In addition to his success on the field, Cam did well in the classroom. More than 40 colleges offered him a **scholarship** to play football and attend college. He chose the University of Florida in Gainesville.

But things didn't go as planned. Newton barely played in his first two years in Florida. He sat behind star quarterback Tim Tebow in 2007

Newton (left) didn't see much action at Florida while backing up Tim Tebow for two years.

and 2008. Then Newton was accused of stealing a laptop computer. That added to his struggles.

Soon Newton left Florida. He soon found success at tiny Blinn College in Brenham, Texas. Newton led Blinn to the 2009 junior college national title.

He passed for 22 touchdowns and ran for 17 more that season. That earned him a scholarship from Auburn University.

Back under the bright lights of big-time college football, Newton blossomed with the Tigers. He showed off his powerful arm. And he was as quick as any running back. He beat defenses by both passing and running. He was strong enough to break tackles. His teammates loved his personality and **leadership**.

Newton emerged as the top quarterback in college football in 2010. He threw 30 touchdown passes, ran for 20 more scores, and even caught a touchdown pass. He led the Tigers to a

Newton holds the Heisman Trophy.

14–0 record and a national title. To top it all off, Newton won the Heisman Trophy. That honor is presented to the best college football player in the country each year. After four years in college, Newton had shown NFL scouts that he was ready for the next step.

CHAPTER 3

TAKING THE NFL BY STORM

In 2011, Carolina Panthers fans became Cam Newton fans in a matter of seconds. Their team chose Newton with the first pick in the NFL **draft**. In training camp, Newton won the job as the team's starting quarterback. Panthers fans soon had plenty of reasons to cheer for their **dynamic** new quarterback.

Cam Newton turned the NFL upside down in his rookie year.

In his first game, Newton shattered an NFL record by passing for 422 yards against the Arizona Cardinals. No player had ever thrown for more yards in his first NFL game.

It was a sign of great things to come. Newton was already among the top quarterbacks in the NFL. When the season ended, he had set rookie records with 4,051 passing yards, 706 rushing yards, and 35 touchdowns. He was an easy choice as the NFL's Offensive Rookie of the Year.

Newton also showed his love for the fans. He has a special bond with kids. He began a tradition of handing a football

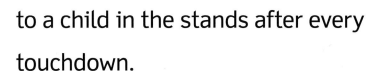
Newton makes a young fan happy by handing him a ball.

to a child in the stands after every touchdown.

He loved to help kids in bigger ways, too. For example, Newton surprised a group of fourth- and fifth-grade students on a class field trip in December 2015.

Newton led the Panthers to a division title in 2013.

He met them at a sporting goods store. First he spoke to the kids. Then he gave each of them a $200 gift card. The children were excited as they picked out gifts. Newton did not **donate** his time and money to make a good impression. He did it because he likes to help kids.

Newton continued to display his talent on the field. But the Panthers were not winning. They posted losing records in each of his first two seasons. That trend did not appear to be changing in 2013 as Carolina lost three of its first four games.

But then the Panthers' offense caught fire. Newton led them to at least 30 points in each of the next four games. He completed an amazing 72 percent of his passes during that stretch. That triggered an eight-game winning streak. Carolina lost only one game the rest of the year. The Panthers lost in the first round of the playoffs. But the best was yet to come.

CHAPTER 4

SUPER SEASON

Cam Newton keeps working, even on his days off. Carolina coach Ron Rivera provided one example in February 2016. He showed the media a sketch board. It was filled with diagrams of plays Newton had seen other teams run. Newton had drawn them up to help prepare for the Super Bowl.

Cam Newton and the Panthers were headed to the Super Bowl in 2015.

But as hard as Newton worked, it was his talent that amazed everyone in 2015. Newton led the charge as the Panthers steamrolled to a 15–1 record. It was one of the greatest seasons in NFL history.

Newton added many plays to his personal highlight reel. He tumbled head-over-heels into the end zone against the Houston Texans. He threw a perfect touchdown pass over the arms of two Indianapolis Colts defenders. And he released another touchdown pass just before a Washington Redskins player clobbered him.

Then there were his amazing numbers. Newton threw five touchdown passes

Newton and the Panthers ran away from the rest of the league in 2015.

in a game three times in one month. He passed for 340 yards and rushed for 100 more against the New York Giants. He threw 21 touchdown passes and just one interception in the entire second half of the season.

A dejected Newton walks off the field after Carolina's Super Bowl loss.

The victory over Arizona put Carolina into the Super Bowl against Denver. Newton struggled in the game. He misfired on his first four passes. He got hit and fumbled the ball near his own goal line. The Broncos recovered it for a touchdown. Newton led a scoring drive in the second quarter, but he never found his stride. In the end, the Panthers lost 24–10.

The year ended badly for Newton. But that could not tarnish his 2015 season. Newton had achieved amazing things both on and off the field that year.

GOING THE EXTRA MILE

Newton's teammates voted him the team's winner of the Ed Block Courage Award in 2015. The honor is presented to one player on each NFL team who displays sportsmanship and courage on and off the field. Newton was singled out for donating money to schools and providing meals for needy people.

CAM NEWTON

- Height: 6 feet 6 inches (198 cm)
- Weight: 260 pounds (118 kg)
- Birth date: May 11, 1989
- Birthplace: Atlanta, Georgia
- Colleges: University of Florida,
    Gainesville (2007–08); Blinn College,
    Brenham, Texas (2009);
    Auburn University (2010–11)
- NFL team: Carolina Panthers, Charlotte,
    North Carolina (2011–)
- Major awards: Heisman Trophy (2010);
    NFL Offensive Rookie of the Year (2011);
    NFL Most Valuable Player (2015)

Charlotte

Atlanta

Auburn

Brenham

Gainesville

FOCUS ON
CAM NEWTON

Write your answers on a separate piece of paper.

1. Write a letter to a friend describing what you learned about Cam Newton.

2. Do you think quarterback would be a fun position to play? Why or why not?

3. When did the Panthers select Newton in the NFL draft?

> **A.** 2009
> **B.** 2011
> **C.** 2015

4. Why did Newton leave the University of Florida?

> **A.** because he wanted more playing time
> **B.** because he was ready for the NFL
> **C.** because he had graduated

Answer key on page 32.

GLOSSARY

discipline
The ability to make oneself do the right thing.

donate
To give away something of value.

draft
A system that allows teams to acquire new players coming into a league.

dynamic
Exciting and energetic.

leadership
The power or ability to lead other people.

scholarship
Money given to a student to pay for education expenses.

varsity
The top team representing a high school or college in a sport or competition.

TO LEARN MORE

BOOKS

Kortemeier, Todd. *Carolina Panthers*. Minneapolis: Abdo Publishing, 2016.

Rogers, Andy. *Who's Who of Pro Football: A Guide to the Game's Greatest Players*. North Mankato, MN: Capstone Press, 2016.

Silverman, Drew. *Today's NFL: 12 Reasons Fans Follow the Game*. North Mankato, MN: 12-Story Library, 2016.

NOTE TO EDUCATORS

Visit **www.focusreaders.com** to find lesson plans, activities, links, and other resources related to this title.

INDEX

Answer Key: 1. Answers will vary; 2. Answers will vary; 3. B; 4. A